FREEDOM'S PROMISE

CAROL
MOSELEY
BRAUN
POLITICIAN AND LEADER

BY DUCHESS HARRIS, JD, PHD
WITH TAMMY GAGNE

Cover image: Carol Moseley Braun was the first African American
woman elected to the US Senate.

Core Library

An Imprint of Abdo Publishing
abdobooks.com

abdocorelibrary.com

Published by Abdo Publishing, a division of ABDO, PO Box 398166, Minneapolis, Minnesota 55439. Copyright © 2020 by Abdo Consulting Group, Inc. International copyrights reserved in all countries. No part of this book may be reproduced in any form without written permission from the publisher. Core Library™ is a trademark and logo of Abdo Publishing.

Printed in the United States of America, North Mankato, Minnesota
022019
092019

THIS BOOK CONTAINS RECYCLED MATERIALS

Cover Photo: Brian Kersey/AP Images
Interior Photos: Brian Kersey/AP Images, 1, 5, 43; Michael Jenkins/Congressional Quarterly/CQ-Roll Call Group/Getty Images, 6–7; Circa Images/Newscom, 9; Dozier Mobley/AP Images, 11; Robert Sherbow/The Life Images Collection/Getty Images, 14–15; Ken Love/AP Images, 17; Arnie Sachs/CNP/Newscom, 19; Chris Kleponis/AFP/Getty Images, 22–23; Fred Jewell/AP Images, 25; Scott Applewhite/AP Images, 27; Red Line Editorial, 29, 33; Doug Mills/AP Images, 30–31; Scott J. Ferrell/Congressional Quarterly/CQ-Roll Call Group/Getty Images, 36–37; Joseph Sohm/Shutterstock Images, 39

Editor: Maddie Spalding
Series Designer: Claire Vanden Branden

Library of Congress Control Number: 2018966003

Publisher's Cataloging-in-Publication Data

Names: Harris, Duchess, author | Gagne, Tammy, author.
Title: Carol Moseley Braun: politician and leader / by Duchess Harris and Tammy Gagne
Other title: Politician and leader
Description: Minneapolis, Minnesota: Abdo Publishing, 2020 | Series: Freedom's promise | Includes online resources and index.
Identifiers: ISBN 9781532118715 (lib. bdg.) | ISBN 9781532172892 (ebook)
Subjects: LCSH: Moseley-Braun, Carol, 1947- --Juvenile literature. | African American women legislators--Biography--Juvenile literature. | African American political activists--Biography--Juvenile literature. | Members of Congress (United States Senate)--Biography--Juvenile literature.
Classification: DDC 328.73092 [B]--dc23

CONTENTS

A LETTER FROM DUCHESS

In 1992 African American politician Carol Moseley Braun ran for the United States Senate. The US Senate is made up of 100 senators. Most of the senators at the time were white men. Moseley Braun wanted the Senate to more closely reflect American society. She argued that all people are supposed to be represented in a democracy. She said, "Our institutions have to reflect the people's concerns."

Moseley Braun won election to the Senate in 1992. She represented the state of Illinois. Until then, a Black woman had never been elected to the Senate. Many women won election to Congress in that year. Because of this, 1992 became known as the "Year of the Woman." Even so, the majority of the people in Congress were still white men.

Moseley Braun accomplished a lot in her five years as US senator. She fought for social change. Join me in learning about Moseley Braun's career and legacy. Follow me on a journey that examines the promise of freedom.

Carol Moseley Braun became a politician because she wanted to help people.

MAKING A DIFFERENCE

Carol Moseley Braun stood in front of a group of US senators. The date was July 22, 1993. Moseley Braun was the first black woman to serve in the US Senate. She had only been a senator for a few months. The people of Illinois had elected her to office the previous fall. But she was already challenging some of the Senate's longest-serving members. The debate at hand was whether to renew a design patent for the United Daughters of the Confederacy (UDC). The UDC was founded in 1894. It preserves Confederate history from the Civil War (1861–1865). Southern senators Jesse Helms

Carol Moseley Braun is a talented public speaker.

and Strom Thurmond supported the renewal. But Moseley Braun did not.

Moseley Braun explained her argument. The UDC's badge featured a Confederate flag. This flag is a symbol of slavery. Moseley Braun explained that this symbol was a painful reminder to all African Americans. Black slaves were once bought and sold like livestock in the United States. During the Civil War, Confederate soldiers fought to keep slavery legal.

AHEAD OF HER TIME

Moseley Braun spoke out against sexual harassment in 1995. More than 20 women had accused Oregon senator Bob Packwood of sexually harassing them. Moseley Braun and five other women senators joined together. They requested public hearings to look into these accusations. The Senate Ethics Committee led an investigation. The investigation took three years. Senators were ready to vote on whether they should expel Packwood from the Senate. Packwood decided to resign instead.

Many African
Americans lived
in Chicago's South
Side in the 1940s.

Moseley Braun then promised to filibuster the proposal. Filibustering means making a lengthy speech to slow down or block lawmaking. It was a brave move for a junior senator. During an early vote, 48 senators had been against the renewal. Fifty senators had supported it. Many who had supported it changed their minds after Moseley Braun's speech. In the final vote, 75 senators were against the renewal. Only 25 still supported it. The Senate killed the proposal.

CHILDHOOD

Carol Elizabeth Moseley was born on August 16, 1947. She grew up in the South Side of Chicago, Illinois.

The South Side is a poor neighborhood in Chicago. Carol's father was a police officer. Her mother worked as a medical technician. They taught Carol that education was important. Carol planned for college while she was in high school. She worked at a post office and local grocery stores to earn money for college.

As a young girl, Carol learned that black people were often treated differently than white people. She became friends with a white girl in her neighborhood.

During the civil rights movement, African Americans protested job discrimination and other mistreatment.

The girl's parents spanked their daughter when they found out she had been playing with a black child.

Prejudice against African Americans was common in the 1950s. The American civil rights movement was just beginning. African Americans struggled to gain equal rights. They protested mistreatment, including job discrimination. Many employers would not hire black people because of the color of their skin.

INSPIRATION

Carol learned that white people who committed crimes against black people often went unpunished. Carol's aunt was killed in a hit-and-run car accident. The white driver was caught but never charged.

Carol's anger about this injustice inspired her to study the law. She wanted to make a difference for other African Americans. She also wanted to make a difference for other women. Women were likewise fighting for equal rights. They faced employment discrimination too. They often were not paid as much as men.

Carol got a political science degree from the University of Illinois at Chicago. She added a law degree from the University of Chicago in 1972. Then she became an assistant US attorney. She worked with federal investigators. She helped bring criminal cases to court. Carol later married Michael Braun. She took his last name and became Carol Moseley Braun.

STRAIGHT TO THE
SOURCE

Moseley Braun said that society has given women and people of color certain roles. She explained the importance of breaking free from these roles:

> *I am convinced that part of the Civil Rights Movement and Women's Rights Movement—the places where they come together—is in the fact that in these times we have really been taking on antique notions of station in life and breaking them down. 'Station' was what relegated women to a particular role, working in the home but not outside the home, being obedient to their husbands. . . . You did not move outside of that place, except at great peril to yourself. The Women's Rights Movement has been pushing at the edge of that envelope. At the same time, the Civil Rights Movement pushed at the edges of the envelope of the 'place' of black people in our society.*

Source: Betty K. Koed. "Interview #3: The 1998 Reelection Campaign." *United States Senate*. United States Senate, April 15, 1999. Web. Accessed October 8, 2018.

What's the Big Idea?
Take a close look at this passage. What connections did Moseley Braun make between the civil rights and women's rights movements? How do you think these movements shaped Moseley Braun's views?

CHAPTER TWO

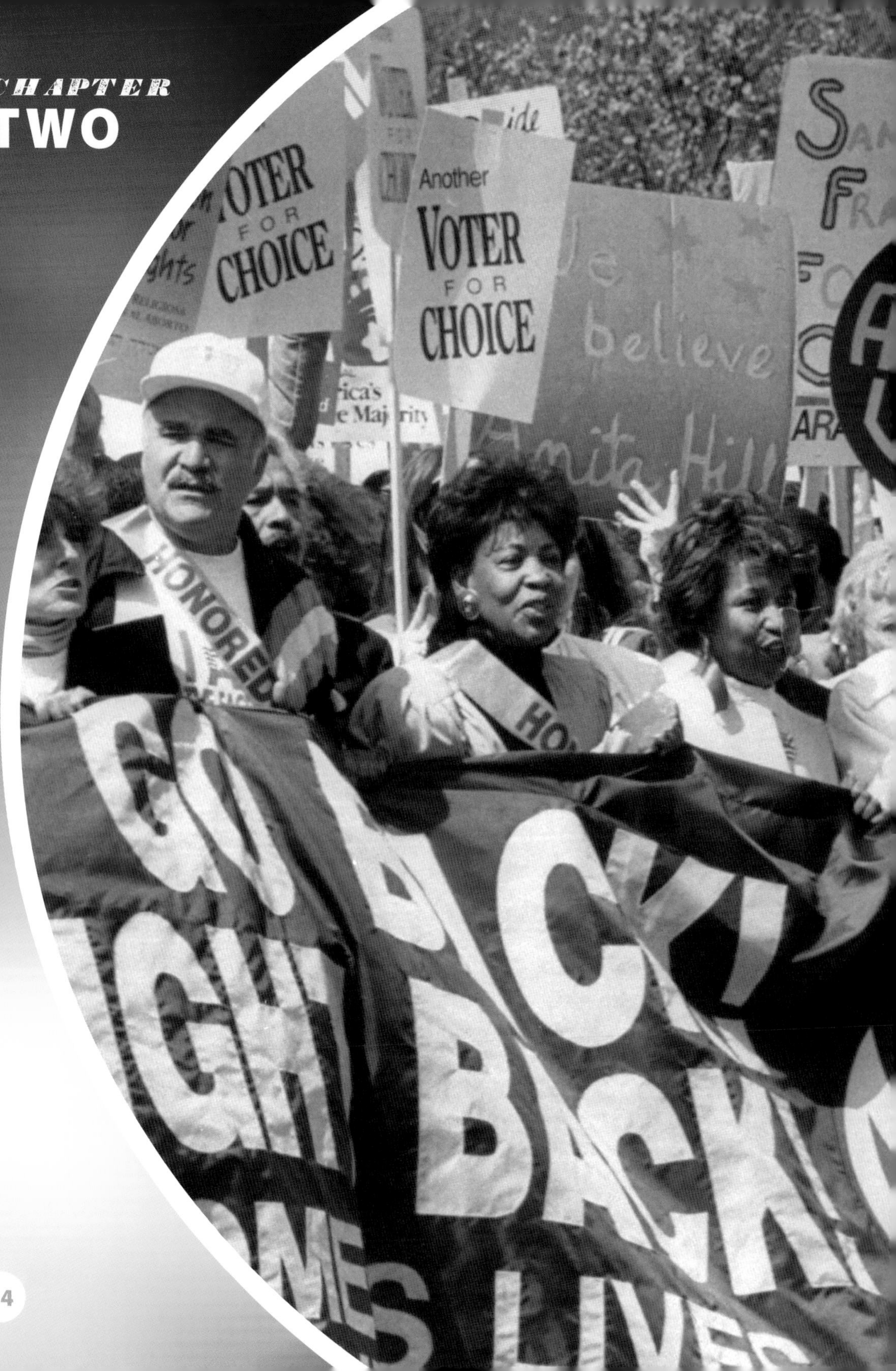

ENTRY INTO POLITICS

M oseley Braun enjoyed helping people. As an assistant US attorney, she prosecuted people who committed crimes against others. After five years in this job, she decided to become a politician. Politicians help change laws. Moseley Braun thought she could make an even bigger difference as a politician.

In 1978 Moseley Braun ran for a seat in the Illinois House of Representatives. She won the race and served as a state representative for ten years. She became the first African American and the first woman to serve as assistant majority leader in the Illinois House.

Moseley Braun, *middle*, supported civil rights and women's rights.

The assistant majority leader has an important job. This person helps unite party members in order to pass laws.

Moseley Braun also worked on other people's political campaigns. These included the campaigns of Richard Newhouse and Harold Washington. Newhouse was the first African American to run for mayor of Chicago. He ran for mayor in 1975. Washington became the first black mayor of Chicago in 1983. He later appointed Moseley Braun as the legislative floor leader. She worked on bills to improve education and ban discrimination in Illinois.

Newhouse and Washington mentored Moseley Braun. Moseley Braun then became a mentor herself. She supported younger African American politicians. In 1985 Mary Flowers was elected to the Illinois House of Representatives. Moseley Braun gave Flowers advice as Flowers got used to her new role.

Moseley Braun supported the careers of Harold Washington, *right*, **and Richard Newhouse,** *middle*.

POLITICAL GOALS

In 1986 Moseley Braun and her husband divorced. Her younger brother died. Her mother had a stroke. Moseley Braun persevered through these difficult times. She planned a new political campaign. She wanted to become the lieutenant governor of Illinois. The lieutenant governor serves as the president of the state Senate. This person presides over debates and votes in the Senate. But Moseley Braun did not get enough support. Moseley Braun was loyal to people who helped her. But she was not afraid to speak her mind when she disagreed with someone. Many people disliked this.

Moseley Braun soon realized that she had little chance of winning the bid for lieutenant governor. She dropped out of the race. But she did not let this setback stop her.

Another opportunity soon arose for Moseley Braun. In 1987 Washington convinced her to run for Cook County's recorder of deeds. This person maintains

Anita Hill testified before the Senate Judiciary Committee on October 11, 1991.

public records relating to property ownership. Moseley Braun won the election. This victory encouraged her to continue pursuing her political goals. She wanted to make a bigger difference in the world of politics.

In 1991 Moseley Braun was following an important hearing in the Senate Judiciary Committee. The committee heard testimony from a black law professor named Anita Hill. The committee was in the middle of confirmation hearings for US Supreme Court nominee

CHRISTINE BLASEY FORD

In 2018 President Donald Trump nominated Brett Kavanaugh as a Supreme Court justice. A woman named Christine Blasey Ford stepped forward. She claimed that Kavanaugh had sexually assaulted her as a teenager. The situation reminded many people of Hill's claims about Thomas. Moseley Braun shared her thoughts in an interview with ABC News. She said that the Senate should not rush Kavanaugh's confirmation. She thought a thorough investigation was needed. But the FBI's investigation lasted only one week. Ford gave her testimony in front of the Senate. Most of the senators voted to confirm Kavanaugh. Kavanaugh became a Supreme Court justice.

Clarence Thomas. Hill had worked for Thomas. She claimed he had sexually harassed her. The Federal Bureau of Investigation (FBI) looked into the matter. But the FBI rushed through the process. Its investigation lasted just three days.

After the hearings, the Senate would vote. Thomas would become a Supreme Court justice if the majority of the senators voted to confirm him. Supreme Court justices rule on important cases that affect the nation's laws. Supreme Court justices do not have term limits. They can remain on the Supreme Court for the rest of their lives.

Moseley Braun watched the hearings closely. The Senate Judiciary Committee was a group of rich white men. Moseley Braun was dismayed when Illinois senator Alan Dixon supported Thomas. She wanted to have a say in future matters in the US Senate. So in 1992, she decided to run for Dixon's seat.

EXPLORE ONLINE

Chapter Two discusses Moseley Braun's early political career. The website below gives more information about this topic. How is the information from the website the same as the information in Chapter Two? What new information did you learn from the website?

CAROL MOSELEY BRAUN
abdocorelibrary.com/carol-moseley-braun

CHAPTER
THREE

SENATE VICTORY

Moseley Braun faced a challenge in running for Dixon's seat. Dixon was popular. Many voters in Chicago's suburbs liked him. By 1992 he had been in the Senate for more than ten years. Politicians who already hold an office have the advantage over new candidates. Presiding politicians have experience performing the job. Voters recognize their names. People are more likely to donate to their campaigns.

Throughout her career, Moseley Braun, *left*, supported other African American politicians.

The race Moseley Braun ran against Dixon was called a Democratic primary. It would determine who would become the Democratic nominee for the US Senate. This race also included another candidate. A wealthy white lawyer named Alfred Hofeld wanted the job as well. Many candidates rely on fundraising to pay for advertising and campaign managers. But Hofeld had money of his own to buy ads. Moseley Braun

Moseley Braun joined presidential candidate Bill Clinton, *left*, on the campaign trail in 1992.

did not have much money. As a result, her campaign was not as well-organized as Hofeld's campaign. Still, she received 38 percent of the votes. She got more votes than either of her opponents. She became the Democratic nominee.

In November 1992, Moseley Braun ran against Republican nominee Richard Williamson. Williamson had more career experience than Moseley Braun. He had worked as a lawyer for two US presidents. Moseley Braun focused her campaign message on the changes she thought Illinois needed. She did not think women or people of color had enough representation in government. Voters liked her message. Fifty-three percent voted for her. She won a spot in the US Senate.

THE YEAR OF THE WOMAN

Moseley Braun was elected to the US Senate in 1992. In that year, the number of women in Congress increased by 69 percent. Congress includes both the Senate and the House of Representatives. The media called 1992 the "Year of the Woman." But Moseley Braun noticed that reporters asked her different questions than they asked male politicians. Journalists often asked her silly things. They asked her about her hair or clothing instead of the issues she cared about. She thought this treatment made women seem less important to the political process than men.

President Bill Clinton, *left*, signed the National Underground Railroad Network to Freedom Act in 1998 while Moseley Braun looked on.

GETTING TO WORK

Senators have important jobs. The US Senate is made up of 100 members. Each state elects two senators. The Senate votes on bills. Bills that are approved by a majority of senators can become law.

Moseley Braun was sworn in as a US senator in January 1993. She understood that her election was historic. She was the first African American woman in the US Senate. But Moseley Braun wanted to be more than a symbol. She wanted to make a difference. She began working to fulfill her campaign promises.

One of Moseley Braun's focuses was health care. She wanted to make changes to the health-care system. She thought every American deserved health-care coverage. She also supported gun control. Crime was high in Chicago, especially in the South Side. Moseley Braun thought that taking guns off the streets would help solve this problem.

Moseley Braun fought for social change and women's rights. Divorced and widowed women were denied access to their husbands' retirement benefits. Moseley Braun introduced bills to change this. In 1994 Moseley Braun worked on the Improving America's Schools Act. This act gave more funding to schools.

Moseley Braun also wanted to preserve African American history for future generations.

MOSELEY BRAUN'S BILLS

Name	Purpose	Year Introduced
Equity in Athletics Disclosure Act	Required colleges and universities to disclose gender participation rates in sports	1993
Partnership to Rebuild America's Schools Act	Provided more federal funding to schools for repair and construction	1997
Comprehensive Women's Pension Protection Act	Gave divorced and widowed women access to their husbands' retirement benefits	1997
National Underground Railroad Network to Freedom Act	Recognized spots along the former Underground Railroad as historic sites	1997

The above chart shows some of the bills Moseley Braun introduced during her time in the US Senate. Based on these bills, what kinds of issues were most important to Moseley Braun?

She created a bill to recognize spots along the former Underground Railroad as historic sites. The Underground Railroad was a network of routes that black people used to escape slavery in the 1800s. Moseley Braun's bill passed in 1998. It is called the National Underground Railroad Network to Freedom Act.

A LONG CAREER

In the US Senate, Moseley Braun served on many committees. Committees handle specific duties. For example, the finance committee deals with issues relating to taxation. Moseley Braun became the first woman to serve on this committee. One issue Moseley Braun took up was the high cost of antiretroviral drugs. People with human immunodeficiency virus (HIV) needed these drugs. These drugs help fight infections. One factor that made the drug prices so high was taxes. The United States taxed drug companies when they brought the ingredients for these medicines into the country. Moseley Braun helped to temporarily remove these taxes.

Moseley Braun, *right*, helped confirm Ruth Bader Ginsburg, *left*, to the US Supreme Court in 1993.

That helped more people with HIV get these lifesaving medications.

SENATE COMMITTEES

In 1993 Moseley Braun joined the Senate Judiciary Committee. Senator Dianne Feinstein of California also joined. They were the first women to serve on this committee. The Senate Judiciary Committee's job is to oversee the Department of Justice. One of the committee's responsibilities is to consider nominees to the Supreme Court.

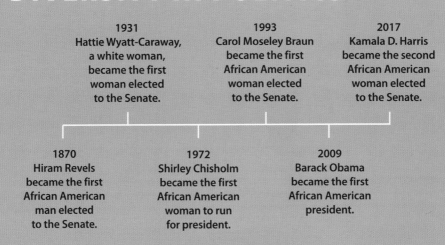

DIVERSITY IN POLITICS

1931
Hattie Wyatt-Caraway, a white woman, became the first woman elected to the Senate.

1993
Carol Moseley Braun became the first African American woman elected to the Senate.

2017
Kamala D. Harris became the second African American woman elected to the Senate.

1870
Hiram Revels became the first African American man elected to the Senate.

1972
Shirley Chisholm became the first African American woman to run for president.

2009
Barack Obama became the first African American president.

The above timeline highlights historic events and politicians in the United States. How does this timeline show the barriers women and people of color face in politics? How do women and people of color continue to shape politics today?

President Bill Clinton appointed Ruth Bader Ginsburg as a Supreme Court nominee. Moseley Braun helped debate Ginsburg's nomination. She supported Ginsburg. At the end of the hearings, Ginsburg was confirmed. She became the second woman to serve as a Supreme Court justice.

CAREER CHANGES

In 1998 Moseley Braun's Senate term ended. She ran for reelection. But she did not win. Clinton appointed

CHANGING THE DRESS CODE

Moseley Braun helped make changes in the US Senate. For many years, women in Congress were expected to wear dresses or skirts. It was not an official rule. But women felt pressured to go along with it. Then Senators Moseley Braun, Nancy Kassebaum, and Barbara Mikulski decided not to play along. They all wore pants on the Senate floor. In response, the Senate changed its unofficial dress code. It allowed women to wear pantsuits.

her to a new post. She was the ambassador to New Zealand and Samoa from 1999 to 2001. She then returned to the United States. She taught political science at DePaul University in Chicago. She also taught at Morris Brown College in Atlanta, Georgia.

In 2003 Moseley Braun ran for president. She thought she had much to offer the country. But many people were not yet willing to take a black woman presidential candidate seriously. Moseley Braun did not gain enough support. She dropped out of the race in 2004. In 2010 she ran for mayor of Chicago but lost. These losses marked the end of her career as an elected official. In 2016 she became a visiting professor at Northwestern University in Evanston, Illinois.

FURTHER EVIDENCE

Chapter Four explores Moseley Braun's career in the Senate. What was one of the main points of this chapter? What evidence is included to support this point? The article at the website below discusses Moseley Braun's experiences and her legacy in the Senate. Find a quote on this website that supports the main point you identified. Does the quote support an existing piece of evidence in the chapter? Or does it offer a new piece of evidence?

A CONVERSATION WITH CAROL MOSELEY BRAUN
abdocorelibrary.com/carol-moseley-braun

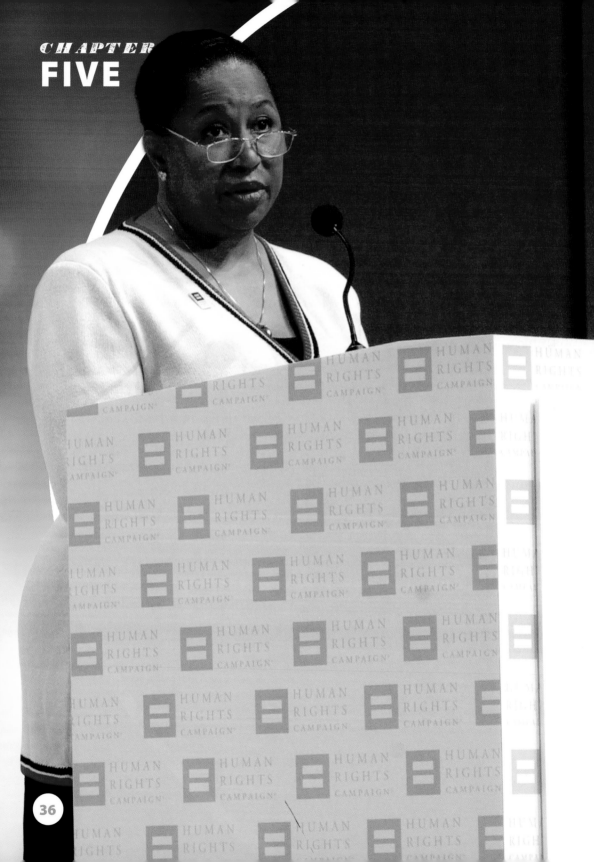

LEGACY

Moseley Braun's election to the Senate helped inspire other black women to pursue careers in politics. Even so, nearly two decades passed before another black woman was elected to the Senate. In 2017 Kamala D. Harris of California was elected to the Senate. Like Moseley Braun, Harris became a member of the Senate Judiciary Committee. Moseley Braun likes the fact that her role in politics has opened doors for others. When she ran for president, she knew she was unlikely to win. But she hoped she could help pave the way for a woman president one day.

Moseley Braun spoke about equality and human rights during a forum in 2003.

SCANDALS

Moseley Braun's campaign for reelection to the Senate was hurt by scandals. One scandal was financial. The federal government limits the amount of money one person can donate to a political campaign. The federal election commission received a claim about Moseley Braun. The claim said that she had accepted donations over the limit. Some reports said that she could not account for $249,000 of her funding. The commission resolved the matter. But it could not erase the stigma that came with the story. As journalist Martin Nichols wrote in the Guardian, "Although the irregularity was later found only to amount to $311, the taint of scandal stuck."

Many black politicians were elected to Congress in 2017. The total number of black Congress members rose to 52 in that year. This was the highest it had ever been.

CIVIL RIGHTS ACTIVIST

Moseley Braun is no longer a senator. But she remains interested in political issues. She supports the Black Lives Matter movement. Black Lives Matter works to end violence

Black Lives Matter activists protest violence against African Americans.

against black people, including violence committed by police. Moseley Braun believes that Black Lives Matter is carrying on the important work of the civil rights movement.

COPING WITH DYSLEXIA

Moseley Braun has dyslexia. People with dyslexia struggle to recognize letters and words. This makes it difficult for them to read. People with dyslexia need support and tutoring. For most of her life, Moseley Braun kept her struggles with dyslexia private. But she later decided to share her story. She urges kids with dyslexia to get the help they need.

Moseley Braun also thinks it is important for black girls to offer their knowledge and talents to the world. She encourages them to be themselves instead of trying to imitate the young white women they see in the media. She tells black girls to value their race and gender. She wants them to see themselves in positive ways. She hopes that they can become role models for future generations of young African Americans.

STRAIGHT TO THE
SOURCE

Moseley Braun remained involved in politics even after she left office. In a 2017 interview, she shared her thoughts on how people can make a difference. She said:

The most important thing you can do is be engaged. People sit back and ask why are things so messed up; it's messed up because you are not doing what you can do. That's the reality and if you get engaged and involved you try to do the best that you can do for others. That is the key. The answer really is you. The inclination for too many people is to sit it out and not to bother because it's too hard. Building [up] others is never easy but it's the key to a better world. I encourage young people again, don't despair because stuff doesn't look right.

Source: "Carol Moseley Braun Talks about Black Lives Matter: 'They Are Following in Some Noble Footsteps.'" *Huffington Post*. Huffington Post, July 19, 2017. Web. Accessed October 8, 2018.

Consider Your Audience

Adapt this passage for a different audience, such as your friends. Write a blog post conveying this same information for the new audience. How does your post differ from the original text and why?

FAST FACTS

- Carol Elizabeth Moseley was born in Chicago on August 16, 1947. Her early experiences with discrimination inspired her to study the law.

- Moseley Braun entered politics in 1978 when she ran for a seat in the Illinois House of Representatives.

- In 1992 Moseley Braun became the first African American woman to be elected to the US Senate. Among the causes most important to her were social issues, women's rights, education, and the environment.

- In 1999 President Bill Clinton appointed Moseley Braun ambassador to New Zealand and Samoa. She later worked as a political science professor at Morris Brown College, DePaul University, and Northwestern University.

- Moseley Braun ran for president in 2003 but dropped out of the race in 2004.

- Moseley Braun helped pave the way for other African Americans to serve in politics.

- Moseley Braun continues to be a civil rights activist today. She supports the Black Lives Matter movement.

AROL ★

R CHICAGO

OSELEY BRAUN FOR MAYOR

43

STOP AND
THINK

Surprise Me

Chapter Four discussed some of Moseley Braun's accomplishments in the Senate. After reading this book, what two or three facts about Moseley Braun's political career did you find most surprising? Write a few sentences about each fact. Why did you find each fact surprising?

Take a Stand

Moseley Braun offered a new perspective when she was elected to the Senate in 1992. She fought for civil rights and women's rights. Do you think it is important to have both women and people of color in government? Why or why not?

Tell the Tale

Chapter One of this book discusses Moseley Braun's successful argument against the United Daughters of the Confederacy's use of the Confederate flag. Imagine that you were in the Senate when Moseley Braun was making her speech. Write 200 words about your experience.

GLOSSARY

ambassador
an official sent to represent his or her country in another nation

design patent
a license to make and own the rights to a particular design

discrimination
the unjust treatment of a person or group based on race or other perceived differences

filibuster
to make a lengthy speech in order to slow down the lawmaking process

nominee
a person who is nominated, or recommended, for something

prejudice
a dislike for a person or group of people based on race or other characteristics

prosecute
to carry out legal action, such as a court trial, against someone accused of a crime

stigma
a feeling of shame or embarrassment about something or someone

ONLINE RESOURCES

To learn more about Carol Moseley Braun, visit our free resource websites below.

Visit **abdocorelibrary.com** or scan this QR code for free Common Core resources for teachers and students, including vetted activities, multimedia, and booklinks, for deeper subject comprehension.

Visit **abdobooklinks.com** or scan this QR code for free additional online weblinks for further learning. These links are routinely monitored and updated to provide the most current information available.

LEARN MORE

Harris, Duchess, with Myra Faye Turner. *Political Resistance in the Current Age*. Minneapolis, MN: Abdo Publishing, 2018.

Winter, Max. *The Civil Rights Movement*. Minneapolis, MN: Abdo Publishing, 2015.

ABOUT THE
AUTHORS

Duchess Harris, JD, PhD

Dr. Harris is a professor of
American Studies at Macalester
College and curator of the Duchess
Harris Collection of ABDO books.
She is also the coauthor of the titles in
the collection, which features popular
selections such as *Hidden Human
Computers: The Black Women of NASA*
and series including News Literacy and
Being Female in America.

Before working with ABDO, Dr. Harris authored several other books
on the topics of race, culture, and American history. She served as an
associate editor for *Litigation News*, the American Bar Association
Section of Litigation's quarterly flagship publication, and was the first
editor in chief of *Law Raza*, an interactive online journal covering race
and the law, published at William Mitchell College of Law. She has
earned a PhD in American Studies from the University of Minnesota and
a JD from William Mitchell College of Law.

Tammy Gagne

Tammy Gagne has written dozens of books for both adults and
children. Her other titles in this series include *The Birth of
Hip-Hop* and *Richard Wright: Author and World Traveler*.
She lives in northern New England with her husband,
son, and menagerie of pets.

INDEX